PAWS

CW00349353

IT'S A PURRFECT DAY

STEVE PLUMMER AND PAT ASHFORTH

SUMMERSDALE

Copyright © Steve Plummer and Pat Ashforth 1997

All rights reserved.

No part of this book may be reproduced by any means, nor transmitted, nor translated into a machine language without the written permission of the publisher.

Summersdale Publishers
46 West Street
Chichester
West Sussex
PO19 1RP
United Kingdom

A CIP catalogue record for this book is available from the British Library.

ISBN 1 84024 018 0

Printed and bound in Great Britain.

PUSS IN BOOTS

CATACOMB

FOOTBALL KITTY

CATAPULT

CAT AS TROPHY

PURROUETTE

PUSSEIDON

PURRJAMAS

CERTIFICAT

PURRSPEX

APURRITION

AL CATONE

CHRISTOPHER COLUMPUSS

EARTHA KITTY

ROMIUW AND MEWLIET

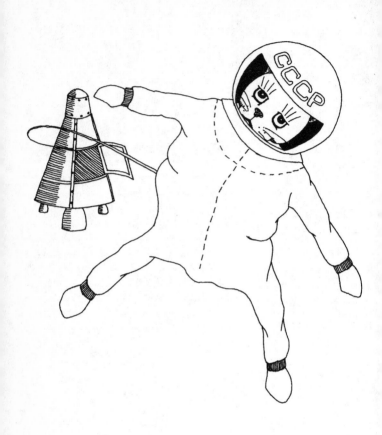

MIOWRIE GARGARIN

THE SOUND OF MIOWSIC

CAT ON A HOT TIN ROOF

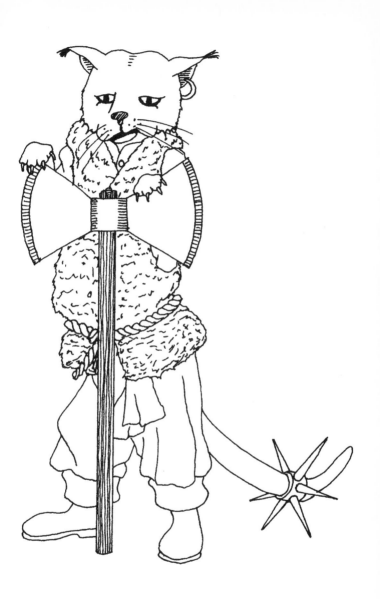

CATILLA THE HUN

SIR ISAAC MEWTON

PYTHAGORPUS

PICATSO

SUPURRMAN

PURRCULES

MEWNICYCLE

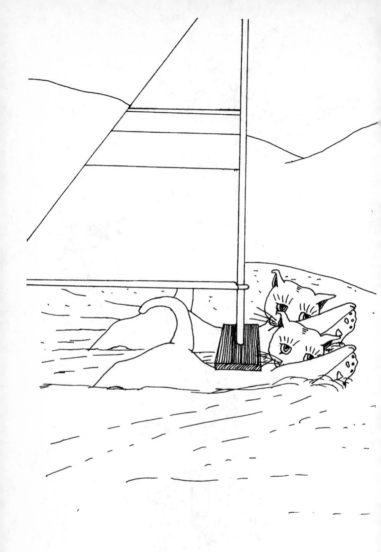

CATAMARAN

PREGNANT PAWS

ACROCATS

MIOWPHONIUM

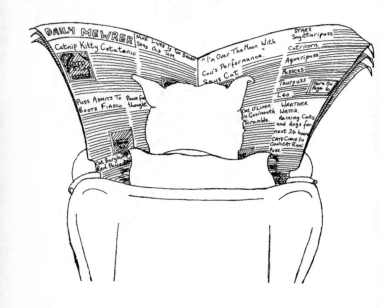

CATCHING UP ON THE MEWS

IMPUSSIBLE

KITTIWAKE

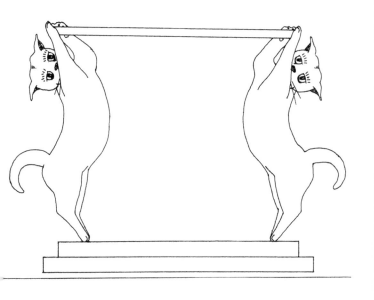

CATERPILLARS

OPURRA HOUSE

This Week

Orphepuss and Mewrydice
starring
Monstercat Caballe
and
Pussydo Domingo

Coming Soon

Purrgy and Bess
***

Joseph and the Amazing Tecnicolour Dreamcat
***

The Miaowkado

MEWSIC EMPURRIUM

PURRCUSSION
DRUM KITS
TOM-TOMS
CATSANETS

MEWPHONIUM
PAW ANGLAIS
MEWKELELE
PURRDY-GURDY

Opuss Catalogue

includes works by

Sibelipuss, Purrcini, Scarcatti,
Miaowzart, Delipuss,
Catcaturian, Purrcell,
Pussorgsky
and Depussy

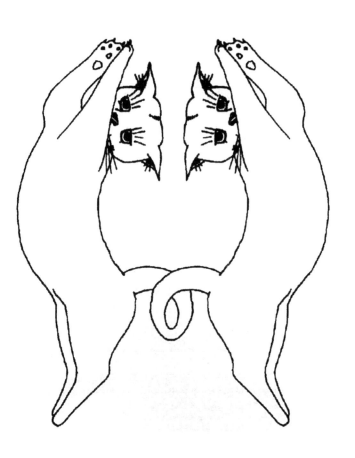

SIAMESE CATS

PURRAMID

QUADRICATERAL

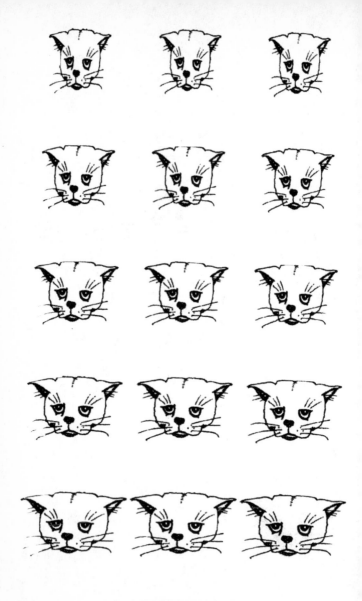

PURRMUTATIONS

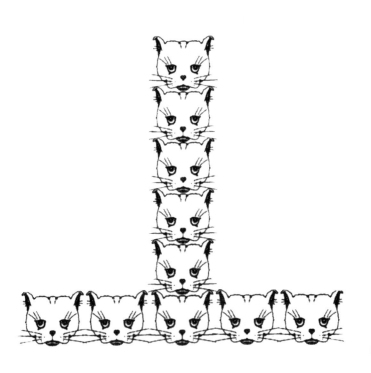

PURRPENDICULR

EQUICATERAL

PURRIMETER

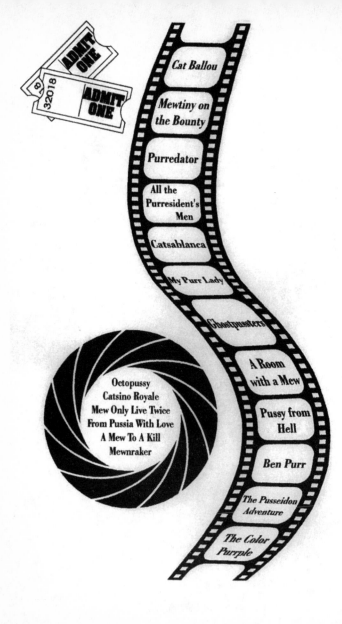

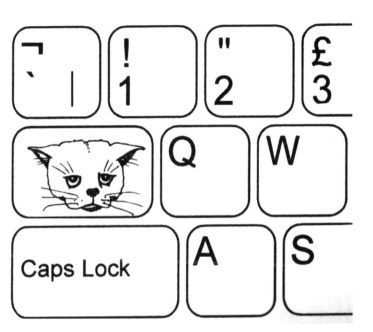

TABBY CAT

Reigning Cats and Dogs

Caterine the Great
The Empurror of Japan
Richard, Cur-de-Lion
Agrippurr
William Woofus
Tiberipuss Caesar
Napoleon Bone-apart
King Charles Spaniel
The Dog of Venice
The Great Danes

The Dramatic Works of
William Shakespurr

❖   ❖   ❖

Antony and Cleocatra
As You Lie Kit
Troilpuss and Cressida
The Taming Of The Mew
Rameow and Mewliet
Corialanpuss
Julipuss Caesar
Titpuss Andronicpuss

MEWNITED NATIONS

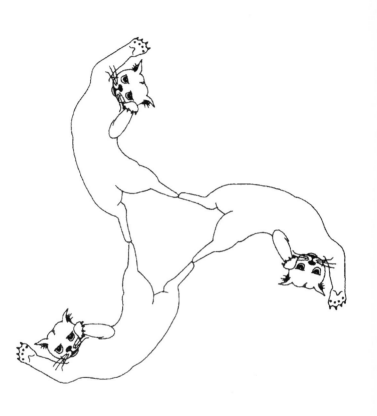

MANX CATS

Where did you get that cat?
If the cat fits wear it
Go cat in hand
I'll eat my cat
A feather in one's cat
Pass the cat round

I take my cat off to you
Cat and gown
Dunce's cat
Old cat
Cats off
Cat trick
Cat and bells
Thinking cat
Cat trick

At the drop of a cat
Keep it under your cat
Wearing my other cat
You're talking through your cat

You can't make a silk puss
out of a sow's ear

Pussession is nine points of the law

How now brown miaow

Play pussom

As stubborn as a mewle
We are not amewsed

Purrls before swine
At cross purrpussies
The cat's purrjamas
All's purr in love and war
10% inspurration, 90% purrspurration

LITERATURE

- PURRADISE LOST
- PURRADISE REGAINED
- THE GREAT CATSBY
- I CLAWDIPUSS
- DAVY CROCKIT
- THE CATTERBURY TALES
- PURRTERHOUSE BLUE
- THE TURN OF THE MEW
- THE OLD CURIOSITY KILLED THE CAT SHOP
- DAVID COPURROFIELD
- OUR MEWTUAL FRIEND
- PURRCULE POIROT

- A MODERN MEWTOPIA
- CATCHER IN THE RYE
- TOM JONES
- TOM THUMB
- TOM BROWN'S SCHOOLDAYS
- TOM SAWYER
- BRAVE MEW WORLD
- SHE
- THE FAIR MAID OF PURRTH
- UNCLE TOM CAT'S CABIN
- HOMAGE TO CATALONIA

- KITTY KITTY BANG BANG
- PAWTRAIT OF A LADY
- PASSAGE TO INDIA
- A ROOM WITH A MEW
- LADY CATTERLEY'S LOVER
- CATS 22
- THE EMPURROR'S NEW CLOTHES
- OLD PUSSUM'S BOOK OF PRACTICAL CATS
- PUSS OF THE D'URBERVILLES
- THE MAYOR OF CATTERBRIDGE
- THE PURR AND THE GLORY

BIG CATS

- THE EYE OF THE TIGER
- THE PINK PANTHER
- PURRIME MINISTERS
- TIGER, TIGER, BURNING BRIGHT
- THE LION, THE WITCH AND THE WARDROBE
- THE LION IN WINTER
- THE PURRESIDENTS OF THE MEWNITED STATES OF AMERICA
- ANDROCLES AND THE LION
- PRIDE AND PREJUDICE
- SANTA CLAWS
- ISAAC MEWTON

PURRSONALITIES

- MADAME PUSSAUD
- SAINT BARTHOLOMEW
- PUSSOLINI
- MIAOW TSE TUNG
- SHERPURR TENZING
- THOMAS TOMPION
- PICATSO
- PINKY & PURRKY
- TRIVIAL PURRSUIT
- CROSSWORD PUSSLES
- ZIGGURCATS & PURRAMIDS
- IMPUSTORS & IMPURRSONATORS

THE MEWNIVERSE

- ESPURRANTO
- CATALAN
- PURRTUGUESE
- CALCATTA
- PURRTO RICO
- PURROSIA
- PURRU

- ALCATRAZ
- CATARACTS
- TOTTENHAM HOTSPURRS
- THE ROYAL MEWS
- THE MEWNITED KINGDOM
- THE CATTY SARK
- MEWSEUMS

- THE MEWSES
- MOUNT OLYMPUSS
- PURRSEPHONE
- OEDIPUSS
- MEWRIPEDES
- ICARPUSS & DAEDALPUSS
- PURRSEUS

NON-FICTION CATEGORIES

- HIPPOPOTAPUSS
- RHINOCERPUSS
- PORPUSS
- OCTOPUSS
- KITTIWAKE
- CATERPILLARS
- PAWCUPINES
- CARNIVORPUSS CREATURES

SCIENTIFIC APPURRATUS

- CLAWSTROPHOBIA
- PURRTASSIUM PURRMANGANATE, PURROXIDES & PHOSPHORPUSS
- MEWNITIONS
- PURRPETUAL MOTION
- THE ROCKET AND OTHER PURRBATECHNICS
- PURRACHUTES
- CATALYTIC CONVERTERS

DUPLICAT

TRIPLICAT

CAT BURGLAR

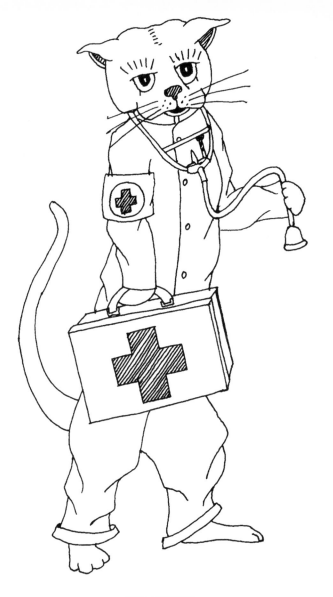

PURRAMEDIC

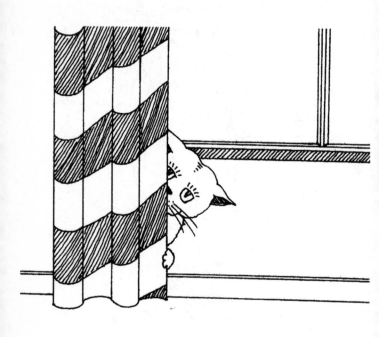

PEEPING TOM

IDENTIKIT

MEOWNTAINEER

THE ROYAL MEWS

PURRENTS